· ONE MORE TIME 4 ·

Every night is Saturday Night!

CONTENTS

Edited by CECIL BOLTON

First Published 1988

Exclusive Distributors
International Music Publications
Southend Road, Woodford Green,
Essex IG8 8HN, England.

Front Cover Photograph reproduced by kind permission of Hollywoods, Romford.

215-2-480

£6.50

Medley 1

ROCK AROUND THE CLOCK

Words and Music by
MAX C. FREEDMAN and JIMMY DAKNIGHT

F

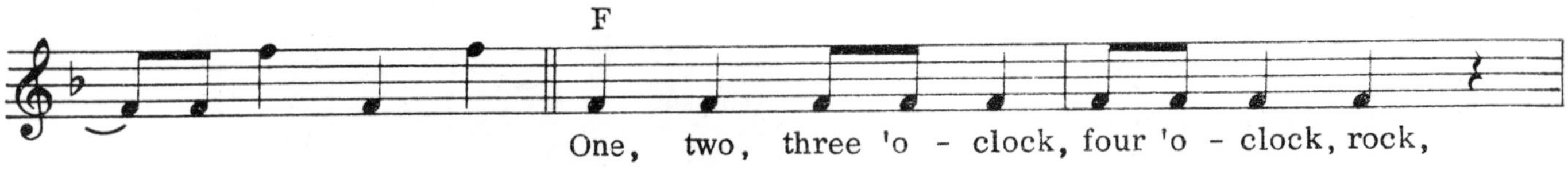
F
One, two, three 'o - clock, four 'o - clock, rock,

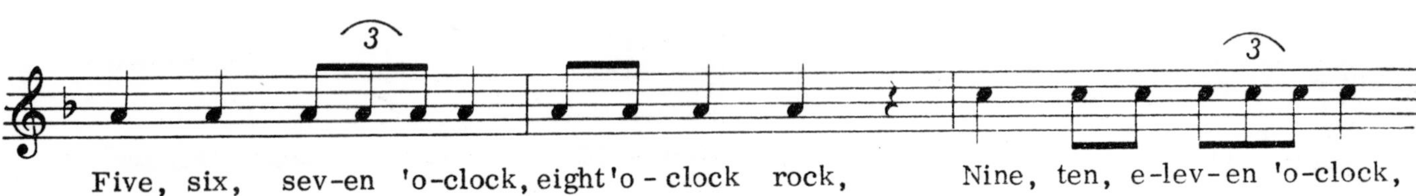
3
3
Five, six, sev-en 'o-clock, eight'o - clock rock, Nine, ten, e-lev-en 'o-clock,

C7
Twelve 'o - clock rock, We're gon - na rock a - round the

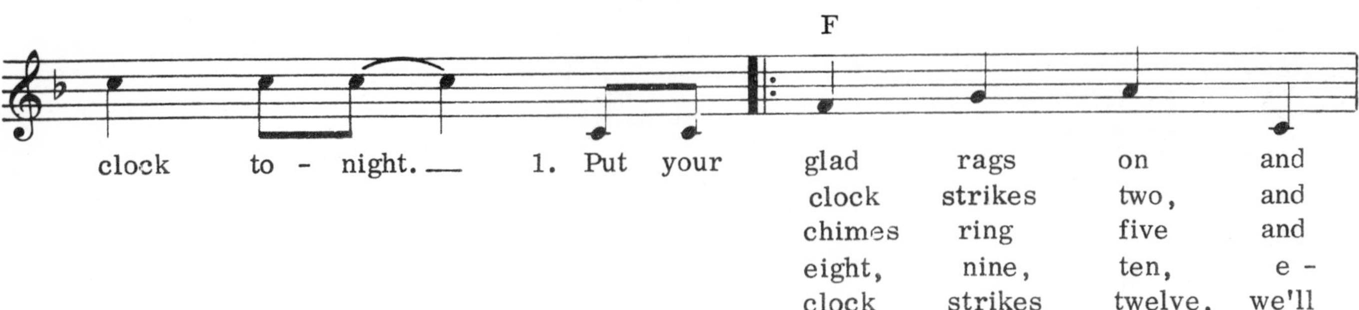
F
clock to - night. — 1. Put your glad rags on and
clock strikes two, and
chimes ring five and
eight, nine, ten, e -
clock strikes twelve, we'll

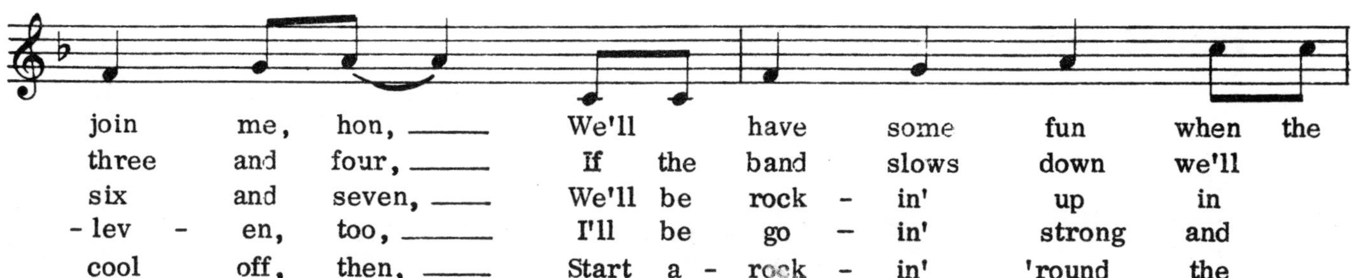
join me, hon, We'll have some fun when the
three and four, If the band slows down we'll
six and seven, We'll be rock - in' up in
- lev - en, too, I'll be go - in' strong and
cool off, then, Start a - rock - in' 'round the

F7
B♭
clock strikes one,
yell for more,
sev - enth heav'n,
so will you,
clock a - gain,
We're gon - na rock a - round the

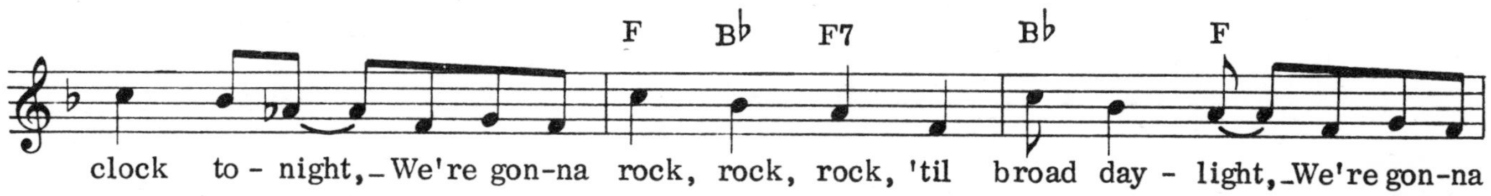
F B♭ F7 B♭ F
clock to - night, We're gon-na rock, rock, rock, 'til broad day - light, We're gon-na

G7 Gm7 C7
rock, gon - na rock a - round the clock to - night.

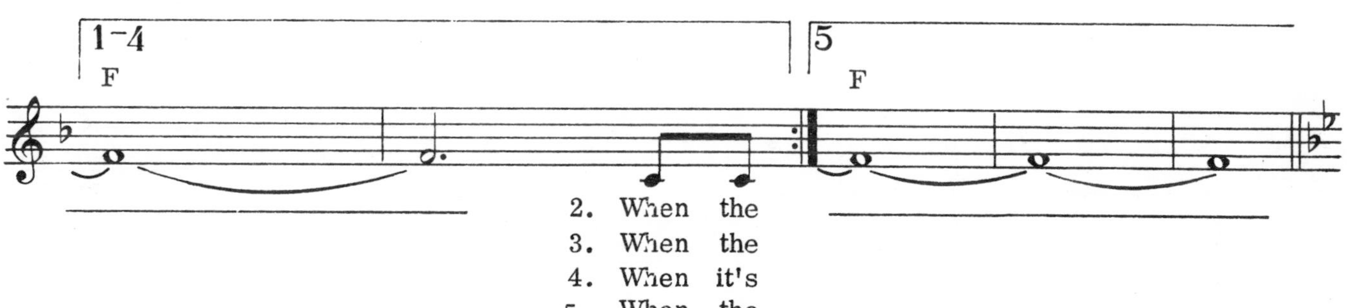
1-4
5
F
F
2. When the
3. When the
4. When it's
5. When the

HOUND DOG

Words and Music by
JERRY LEIBER and MIKE STOLLER

E♭7
B♭
You ain't noth - in' but a Hound Dog, ___ cry-in' all the
time. You ain't noth - in' but a Hound Dog, ___
___ cry - in' all the time. Well, ___ you ain't
F7
E♭7
nev-er caught a rab -bit and you ain't no friend ___ of mine.
no chord
When they said you was high - classed, well, that was just a
lie. When they said you was high - classed,
Well, that was just a lie. Well, ___ you ain't
1 B♭
nev-er caught a rab -bit and you ain't no friend ___ of mine.
2 B♭
You ain't noth - in' but a mine. ___

041

Medley 2

LOVE LETTERS IN THE SAND

Words by NICK KENNY and CHARLES KENNY
Music by J. FRED COOTS

C7 Gm7 C7 F C7
On a

F D♭7 Gm G7
day like to - day, We passed the time a - way, Writ - ing

C7 G7 C7 F C7
love let - ters in the sand. ——— How you

F D♭7 Gm G7
laughed when I cried, Each time I saw the tide take our

C7 G7 C7 F C E7
love let - ters in the sand. ——— You made a

A7 Dm B♭
vow that you would al - ways be true, —— But some-

G7 Gm7 C7
-how that vow meant noth - ing to you. —— Now my

F D♭7 Gm G7
poor heart just aches with ev - 'ry wave that breaks ov - er

C7 Gm7 C7 F D7
love let - ters in the sand.

WHO'S SORRY NOW

Words by HARRY RUBY and BERT KALMAR
Music by TED SNYDER

G
B7
Who's sor - ry now? Who's sor - ry now?

E7
A7
Whose heart is ach - ing for break - ing each vow?

D7
G
E
Who's sad and blue? Who's cry - ing too?

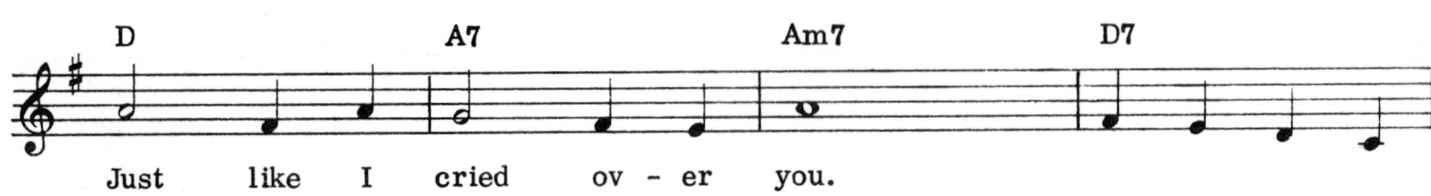
D
A7
Am7
D7
Just like I cried ov - er you.

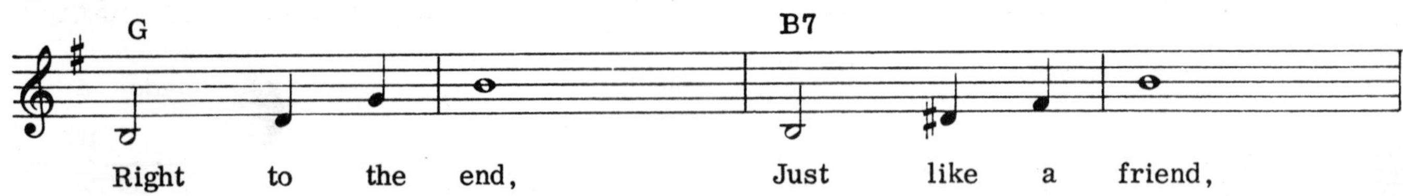
G
B7
Right to the end, Just like a friend,

E7
Am
E7
I tried to warn you some - how.

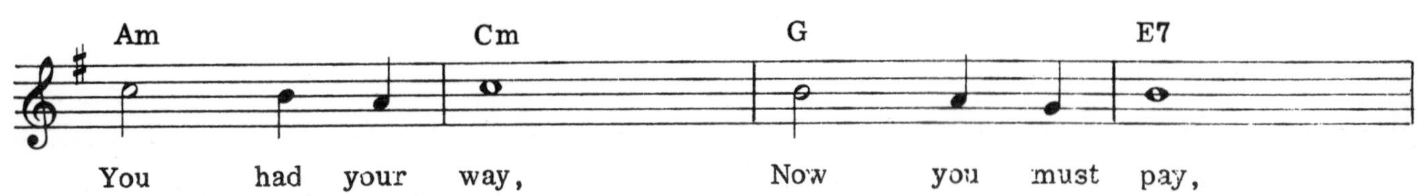
Am
Cm
G
E7
You had your way, Now you must pay,

Am
D7
G
G7
I'm glad that you're sor - ry now.

DIANA

Words and Music by
PAUL ANKA

C Am Dm7 G7
I'm so young and you're so old, This my dar - ling I've been told.
C Am Dm7 G
I don't care just what they say, 'cause for ev - er I will pray,
C Am Dm7 G7 C
You and I will be as free as the birds up in the trees. Oh
Am Dm7 G7 C
please stay by me, Di - an - a.
C Am Dm7 G7
Thrills I get when you hold me close, Oh my dar - ling you're the most.
C Am Dm7 G
I love you but do you love me? Oh Di - an - a can't you see,
C Am Dm7 G C
I love you with all my heart, and I hope we will nev-er part, Oh
Am Dm7 G C C
please stay with me, Di - an - a. Oh
Am7 Dm7 G7 C E F
please stay with me, Di - an - a. If your

CRY

Words and Music by
CHURCHILL KOHLMAN

B♭m F E F B♭m F7 E F A
sweet-heart sends a let - ter of good - bye, It's no
Dm D7
se - cret you'll feel bet - ter if you cry. When
Gm7 Gm7 C F D7
wak - ing from a bad dream don't you some - times think it's real? But it's
G7 E F G7 Gm7 C7 E F
on - ly false e - mo - tions that you feel! If your
B♭m F E F B♭m F7 E F A
heart-aches seem to hang a - round too long, And your
Dm D7
blues keep get-ting blu - er with each song, Re -
Gm7 F D7
-mem - ber, sun-shine can be found be - hind a cloud-y sky, So let your
G7 rit. Gm7 C7 F / B♭ / F
hair down and go on and cry.

Medley 3

ONLY YOU

Words and Music by
BUCK RAM and ANDE RAND

Ab Fm Bbm D♮ Eb Ab
On - ly you can make this

C7 Fm
world seem right, On - ly you can make the

Ab7 Db Eb
dark - ness bright, On-ly you, and you a - lone can

Ab C7 Fm Bb7
thrill me like you do, and fill my heart with love for on-ly you.

Eb7 D♮ Eb Ab
On - ly you can make this

C7 Fm
change in me, For it's true you are my

Ab7 Db
des - ti - ny. When you hold my hand, I

Dbm Ab F7
un - der-stand the mag - ic that you do, You're my dream-

Bb7 Eb7 Ab
come true, my one and on-ly you. My

MY PRAYER

English Lyrics by JIMMY KENNEDY
Music by GEORGES BOULANGER

D♭ (D♭°)
prayer is to lin-ger with you, At the end of the
G♭m D♭ A♭7
day, in a dream that's di - vine. My
D♭ (D♭°)
prayer is a rap-ture in blue, With the world far a-
G♭m A♭ D♭
-way, and your lips close to mine. To-
G♭m D♭m
- night while our hearts are a - glow, Oh,
G♭m7 E♭m7 A♭7
tell me the words that I'm long-ing to know. My
D♭ (D♭°)
prayer and the ans-wer you give, May they still be the
G♭m D♭
same, for as long as we live, That you'll al-ways be
E♭m7 A♭7 D♭
there, at the end of my prayer. I saw the

HARBOUR LIGHTS

Words by JIMMY KENNEDY
Music by WILHELM GROSZ

B♭7 D E♭
Har - bour Lights, They on - ly told me we were part - ing,
B♭ Fm B♭7 E♭
The same old Har - bour Lights That once brought you to me.
B♭7
I watched the Har - bour Lights, How could I help if tears were
D E♭ B♭ Fm B♭7
start - ing? Good - bye to ten - der nights, Be-side the sil-v'ry
E♭ / A♭ / E♭ A♭ A♭m
sea. I longed to hold you near and kiss you just once
E♭ F7
more, But you were on the ship and I was on the
B♭7 E♭ B♭7
shore. Now I know lone - ly nights,
D E♭
For all the while my heart is whis - p'ring, Some oth - er
B♭7 E♭ Dm7 G7
Har - bour Lights will steal your love from me. Oh,

THE GREAT PRETENDER

Words and Music by
BUCK RAM

C G C C7 F
yes, — I'm the great pre - ten - der, — Pre - tend - in' that I'm — do - in'
C C7 F G C F Dm
well; My need is such, — I pre - tend too much, I'm
C Dm G7 C C G7
lone - ly but no - one can tell. Oh, yes, — I'm the great pre-
C C7 F C
-ten - der, — A - drift in a world — of my own; I
F G C F C Dm G7
play the game — but, to my real shame, You've left me to dream — all a-
C F C
-lone. Too real — is this feel - ing of make - be - lieve, Too
F C G7 C G7
real — when I feel — what my heart — can't con-ceal, Oh, — yes, — I'm the great pre-
C F C
-ten - der, — Just laugh - in' and gay — like a clown; I
F G C F Dm C Dm7 G7
seem to be — what I'm not, you see, I'm wear-in' my heart — like a
E F C Dm7 G7 C / F / C
crown; Pre - tend-in' that you're — still a - roun'. —

Medley 4

JAILHOUSE ROCK

Words and Music by
JERRY LEIBER and MIKE STOLLER

F
D♭7
C7
mf
1. The
war - den threw a par - ty in the coun - ty jail, — The
2. Spi - der Mur - phy play'd the ten - or sax - o - phone, –
3. Num - ber For - ty - sev - en said to Num - ber Three, –
E
pri - son band was there and they be - gan to wail. — The
Lit - tle Joe was blow - in' on the slide trom - bone. — The
"You're the cut - est jail - bird I ev - er did see. — I
band was jump - in' and the joint be - gan to swing, — You
drum - mer boy from Il - li - nois went crash, boom, bang! — The
sure would be de - light - ed with your com - pa - ny. — Come
should - 've heard those knock - out jail - birds sing. —
whole — rhy - thm sec - tion was the pur - ple gang. —
on and do the Jail - house Rock with me." —
Let's
B♭7
rock!
Let's rock!
Ev - 'ry - bo - dy in the whole cell block — was a
danc - in' to the Jail - House Rock! —
1. 2.
3.

THE LOCO-MOTION

Words and Music by
GERRY GOFFIN and CAROLE KING

Eb
Cm
Eb
C'm on, ba-by, do
Ev-'ry-bod-y's do - in' a brand new dance now.

Cm
The Lo-co-Mo - tion.
Eb
Cm
I know you'll get to like it if you give it a chance now.

Eb
C'm on, ba-by, do
Cm
The Lo-co-Mo - tion.
Ab
My lit-tle ba-by sis - ter can

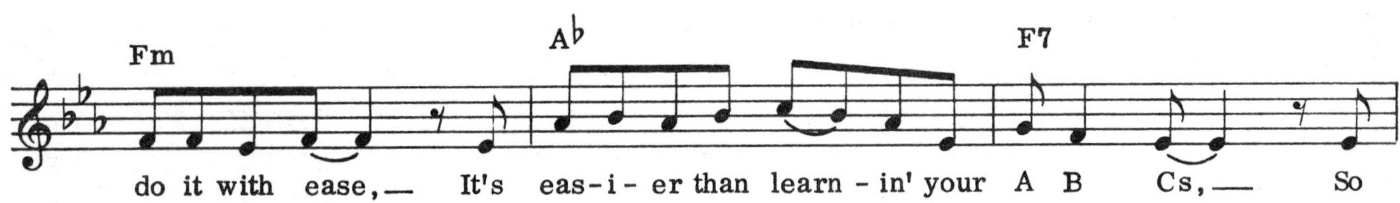
Fm
Ab
F7
do it with ease, It's eas-i- er than learn - in' your A B Cs, So

Eb
Bb9
Eb
come on, come on, do The Lo-co-Mo-tion with me. You got - ta

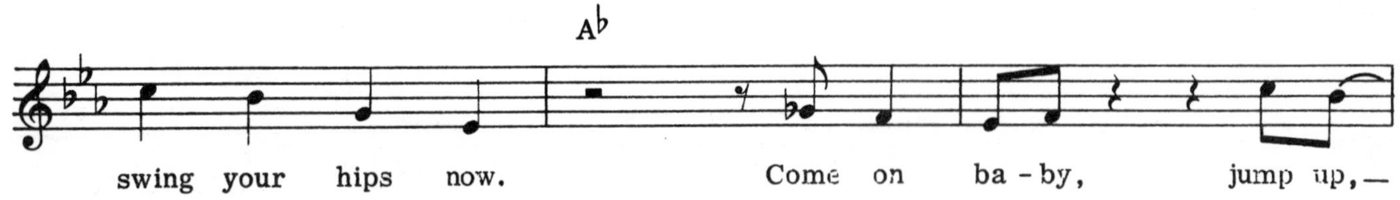
Ab
swing your hips now. Come on ba - by, jump up,

Eb
Bb7
jump back, Oh well, I think you got the knack.

Eb
Cm
Now that you can do ___ it let's make a chain ___ now,
Move a - round the floor ___ in a Lo - co - Mo - tion,
Eb
C'm on, ba - by, do ___
Cm
The Lo - co - Mo - tion.
A
Eb
Cm
chug - a - chug - a mo - tion like a rail - road train, ___ now.
Do it hold - in' hands ___ if ___ you get the no - tion.
Eb
C'm on, ba - by, do ___
Cm
The lo - co - Mo - tion.
There's
Ab
Fm
Do it nice and eas - y now, don't lose con - trol, ___ A
nev - er been a dance ___ that's so eas - y to do, ___ It
Ab
F7
lit - tle bit of rhy - thm and a lot of soul. ___ ___
ev - en makes you hap - py when you're feel - in' blue ___ So
Eb
Bb9
Come on, come on, do ___ The Lo - co - Mo - tion with
come on, come on, do ___ The Lo - co - Mo - tion with
Eb
C'm on, ba - by, do ___
Cm
The Lo - co - Mo - tion
me.
me.
C'm on, ba - by, do ___
C
The Lo - co - Mo - tion.
Eb
Well

ROCKIN' ALL OVER THE WORLD

Words and Music by
JOHN FOGERTY

C
F7
here we are and here we are and here we go, On and on and we're
C
G
hit-tin' the road, here we go, Rock-in' all o - ver the world.
C
C
1. Well, gid-dy up and gid-dy up and
gon-na tell your mam-ma what you're
F7
get a - way, We're go - ing cra - zy and we're go - ing to - day. Here we go
gon-na do. Come on a - round and get your danc - ing shoes, Here we go
C
G
C
Rock-in' all o - ver the world.
C
And I like it, I like it, I like it, I like it, I la
F7
C
la la like it. La la la la Here we go.
G
C
1
Rock - in' all o - ver the world.
2. I'm

2
C
F7
And I like — it, I like — it, I like — it, I like — it, I la —
(F#o)
C
G
— la la like — it, La — la la la, — Here we go, — Rock-
C
- in' all — o - ver the world. — And I like —
C
F7
— it, I like — it, I like — it, I like — it, I la — la la like — it. La —
C
G
— la la la — Here we go, — Rock-in' all o - ver the world. —
C
C
And I like — it, I like — it, I like —
F7
(F#o)
— it, I like — it, I la — la la like — it, La — la la la, — Here we go, —
C
G
C
— Rock - in' all — o - ver the world. —

Medley 5

LIVING DOLL

Words and Music by
LIONEL BART

C
F7
C

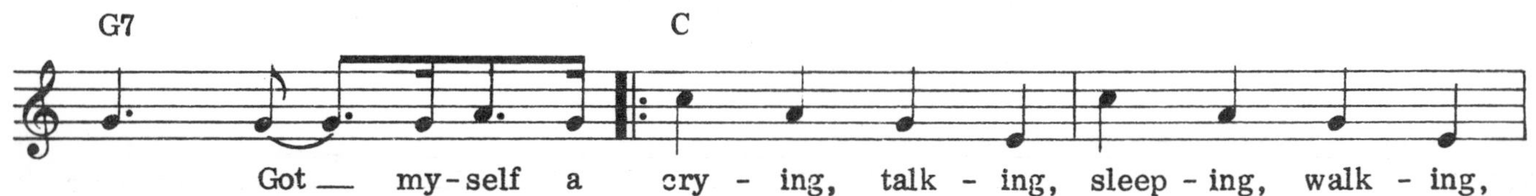
G7
C
Got — my-self a cry - ing, talk - ing, sleep - ing, walk - ing,

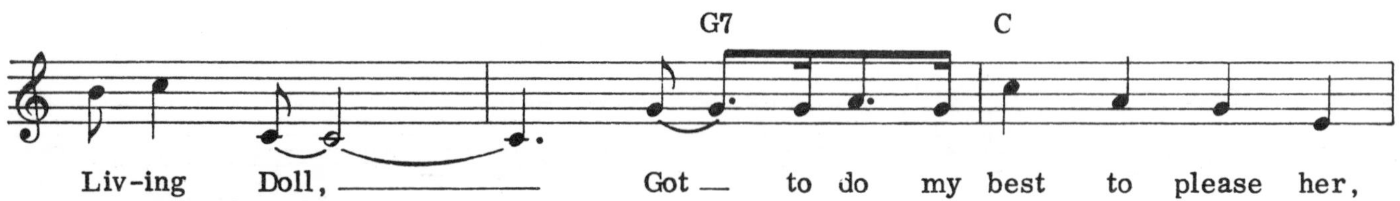
G7
C
Liv-ing Doll, — Got — to do my best to please her,

D7
G7
just 'cos she's a Liv - ing Doll. — Such — a rov - ing

C
A7
eye, and that is why she sat - is - fies my soul, —

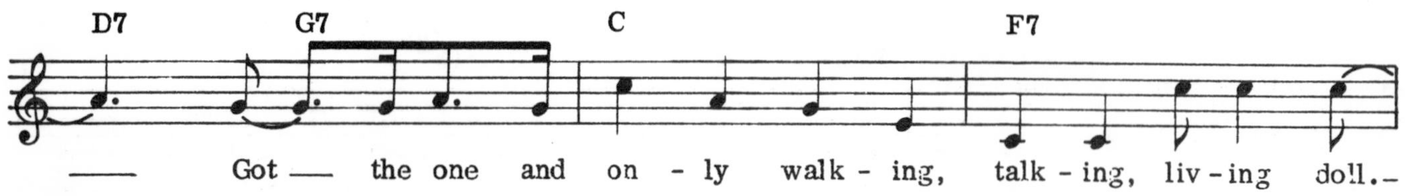
D7
G7
C
F7
— Got — the one and on - ly walk - ing, talk - ing, liv - ing doll. —

1
2
C
G7
C
C7
Got — my-self a
The

THE YOUNG ONES

Words and Music by
ROY BENNETT and SID TEPPER

F Dm
young— ones, —— Darl-ing we're the young— ones, —— And
-mor - row, —— Why wait 'till to-mor - row, —— To-
F Dm7 F
young— ones —— should-n't be a-fraid, —— To live,
-mor - row —— some-times ne-ver comes. —— So love,
C7 F B♭ F
love, while the flame— is strong, — For we won't be the
me, there's a song to be sung, — And the best time is to
C7 1 F C7 2 F B♭
young ones ve-ry long. —— To- young. —— Once in ev-'ry life-time
sing it while we're
F G
comes a love like this. I need you and you need me,
C7 F
Oh my darl-ing can't you see, — Young — dreams —— should be dreamed to-
Dm F
-geth - er, —— And young— hearts, —— should-n't be a-
Dm7 F C7 F
-fraid, —— And some day when the years— have flown,
B♭ F C7 F G7
—— Darl-ing this we'll teach the young ones of our own.

023
024

BACHELOR BOY

Words and Music by
BRUCE WELCH and CLIFF RICHARD

C
F
Dm7
G7
When I was young — my fath - er said "Son I have

C
C
some - thing to say." ——
And what he told me I'll

F
Dm7
G7
C
nev - er for - get un - til my dy - in' day.

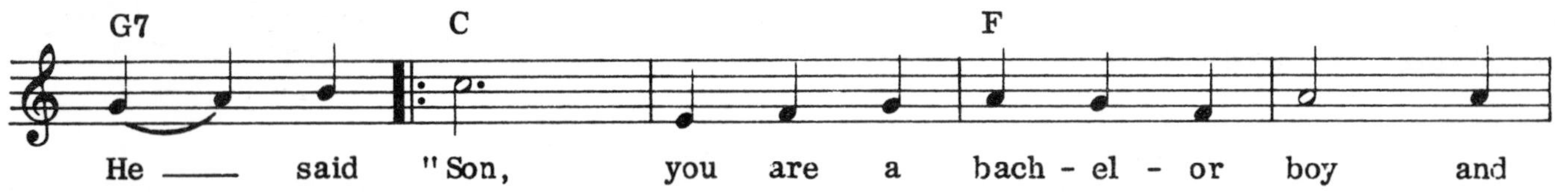

G7
C
F
He — said "Son, you are a bach - el - or boy and

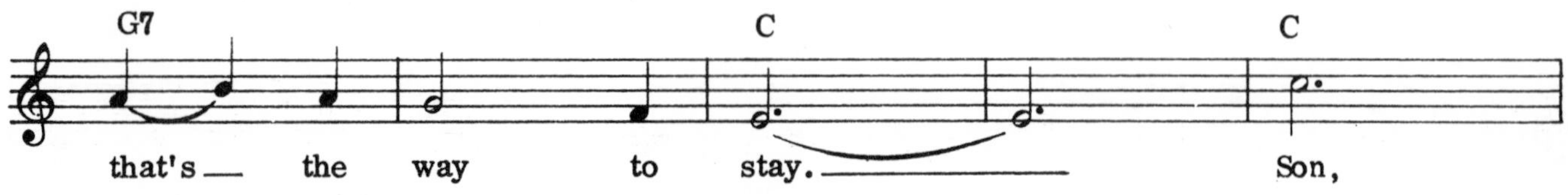

G7
C
C
that's — the way to stay. ——
Son,

F
G
you be a bach - el - or boy un - til your dy - in'

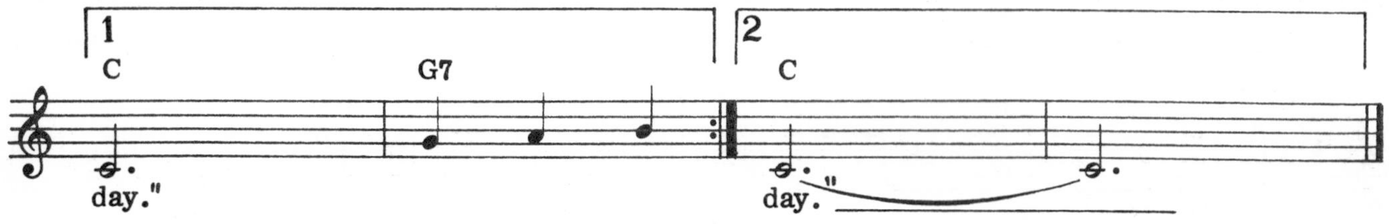

1
C
G7
day."
2
C
day." ——

Medley 6

HANDFUL OF SONGS

Words and Music by
MICHAEL PRATT, TOMMY STEELE
and LIONEL BART

I've got a hand-ful of songs to sing— you, Can't stop my voice when it
More-ov-er wher-ev-er we may roam— to, Or an-y shore where we
longs to sing— you, New songs, and blue songs and songs to bring— you
may be blown— to, We'll know that we're gon-na feel at home— to
hap-pi-ness, — no more, no less.—
La Bel-la — Mus-i-ca. —
Jazz — and cha cha cha, — Ca-lyp-sos and street ven-dors cries.
Strains of old re-frains, — sleep-y time ba-by lul-la-bies.—
I've got a hand-ful of songs to sing-you, I've got a heart-ful of love to bring-you,
True love for you love, and love's a thing-you keep, — So here's a
hand-ful of songs — go-ing cheap. To spend one

THAT'S MY DESIRE

Words and Music by
CARROLL LOVEDAY and HELMA KRESA

C G7 Dm7
night with you in our old ren - dez-vous, And rem - in-
G7 Dm7 C
-isce with you, That's my de - sire. To meet where
C G7 D7
gyp - sies play, down in that dim ca - fe, And dance till
G7 Dm7 G7 C / F / C
break of day, That's my de - sire. We'll sip a
F G7 C
lit-tle glass of wine, I'll gaze in - to your eyes di - vine, I'll feel the
D7 G7 / Dm7 / G7 C
touch of your lips press-ing on mine; To hear you
G7 D7
whis - per low just when it's time to go, "Che - rie, I
G7 Dm7 G7 C G7
3 3 3 3
love you so", That's my de - sire. You

I HEAR YOU KNOCKIN'

Words and Music by
DAVE BARTHOLOMEW and PEARL KING

C
went a-way and left me long time a - go,— Now you come back knock-in'
told you way back a long time a - go,— The day would come when you'd
F7
at my door— I hear— you knock - in' — but you can't — come
miss me so—
C F7
in, — I hear— you knock - in' —
G
go back where— you've been. —
I
You
C
begged you not to go but you said good-bye,— Now you come back tell - in'
bet - ter go back to your 'used to be',— Be - cause your love's no
F7
all those lies— I hear— you knock- in' — but you can't — come
good to me—
C F7
in, — I hear—you knock - in' —
1
G
go back where — you've been. — 2. I
2
F7 G7 C
I know where — you've been. —

Medley 7

ARE YOU LONESOME TONIGHT

Words and Music by
ROY TURK and LOU HANDMAN

Am7 D7 Am7 D7 Am7 D7 G Am7 D7
Are you
G
lone - some to - night, Do you miss me to - night, Are you
E7 Am
sor - ry we drift - ed a - part? Does your
Am D7
mem - o - ry stray To a bright sum - mer day, When I
Am7 D G
kissed you and called you "Sweet-heart? Do the
G7 C
chairs in your par - lour seem emp - ty and bare, Do you
A7 A7 D A7 D
gaze at your door - step and pic - ture me there? Is your
G G7 A7
heart filled with pain? Shall I come back a - gain? Tell me
Am7 D7 Am7 D7 Am7 D G G7
dear, Are you lone - some to - night?

TEARS
Words by FRANK CAPANO
Music by BILLY URH
C D7
Tears for sou - ven - irs are all you left me,
G7 C
Mem - 'ries of a love you nev - er meant.
A A7 D7
I just can't be - lieve you could for - get me,
D7 G7
Af - ter all the hap - py hours we spent to - geth - er.
C D7
Tears have been my on - ly con - so - la - tion, But tears can't
G7 E
mend a bro - ken heart I must con - fess. Let's for -
F (G) C A7 A
-give and for - get, Turn our tears of re - gret, Once
D G7 C D
more to tears of hap - pi - ness. I

059

TRUE LOVE

Words and Music by
COLE PORTER

G
C
(A7)
G°
G
give to you and you give to me,
D7
C
G
True love, true love. So, on and
C
(A7)
G°
G
D7
on it will al - ways be, True love,
G
Cm
F7
true love. For you and I have a
B♭
G7
Cm
F7
guard - ian an - gel on high with noth - ing to
B♭7
D7
G
C
(A7)
G°
do, But to give to you and to give to
G
D7
G
me, Love for - ev - er true,
Am7
D7
G
Love for - ev - er true.

Medley 8

CHANSON D'AMOUR (SONG OF LOVE)

Words and Music by
WAYNE SHANKLIN

D Bm Em7 A7 Em7 A7
D E7 Em7
Chan - son d'a - mour Ra da da da
A7 D F♯7 B7
da, Play en - core. Here
Em A7
in my heart, Ra da da da da,
D Em7 A7 D E7
More and more. Chan - son d'a -
Em7 A7
- mour, Ra da da da da, Je t'a-dore
D F♯7 B7 Em
Each time I hear
A7 D
Ra da da da da chan-son chan- son d'a - mour
A7 D B♭7
Ev-'ry- time I hear chan-son chan-son d'a-mour.

HAPPINESS

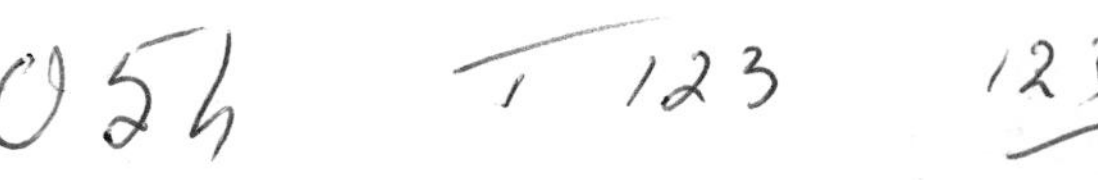

Words and Music by
BILL ANDERSON

CHORUS

Eb Ab Bb7

Hap-pi - ness, — hap-pi - ness, — the great-est gift — that

Eb Ab

I pos- sess, — I thank the Lord — that I've been blessed — with

Bb Eb

more than my share of hap - pi - ness. — To

VERSE

Eb

me this world is a

Ab Bb Eb

won-der - ful place, I'm the luck-i - est hu - man in the hu- man race, — I've

Eb
Ab
Bb7
Eb
got no sil-ver and I've got no gold, But I've got hap-pi-ness in my soul.

CHORUS
Eb
Ab
Bb7
Hap-pi - ness, — hap-pi - ness, — the great-est gift — that

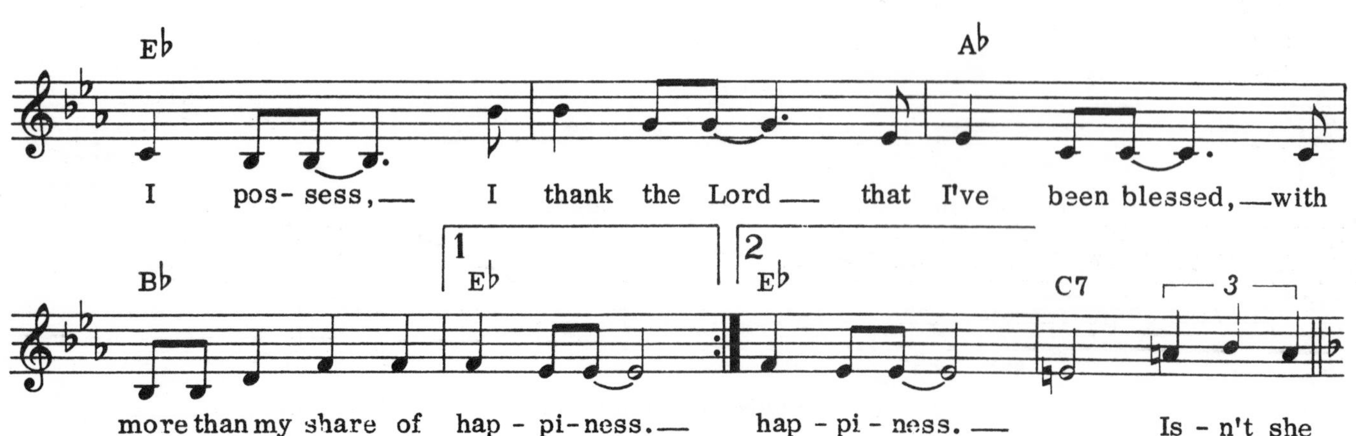
Eb
Ab
I pos- sess, — I thank the Lord — that I've been blessed, — with
Bb
1
Eb
2
Eb
C7
3
more than my share of hap - pi-ness. — hap - pi - ness. — Is - n't she

ISN'T SHE LOVELY

Words and Music by
STEVIE WONDER

Dm G7 3 B♭
love - ly, is - n't she won - der ful?
pret - ty, tru - ly the an - gel's best?
love - ly, life and love are the same.
F 3 Dm7 G7 3
Is - n't she pre - cious, less than one
Boy I'm so hap - py, we have been
Life is A - i - sha, the mean-ing
B♭ F 3 B♭
min - ute old? I nev - er thought through love we'd be
heav - en blessed. I can't be - lieve what God has done,
of her name. Lon-die, it could have not been done
A7 3 Dm7 G7 3
mak - ing one as love-ly as she. But is - n't she
through us He's giv-en life to one. But is - n't she
with - out you who con-ceived the one. That's so ve - ry
Dm7 C7 F / B♭ /
love - ly,
love - ly,
love - ly,
made from love?
1-2 F 3
2. Is - n't she
3. Is - n't she
3 F B♭ 3 F

Medley 9

LET'S TWIST AGAIN

Words and Music by
KAL MANN and DAVE APPELL

G Am7 D G Am7 D Am7/D
Let's
G B7 Em
Twist a-gain like we did last Sum-mer, Yea, Let's
Am7 D7 Am7
Twist a-gain like we did last year. Don't-cha re-
G B7 Em
-mem-ber when things were real-ly hum-min', Yea, Let's
Am7 D7 G C G
Twist a-gain, Twist-in' time is here. Ee - ah
C G
Round 'n-a round 'n-a up-'n down we go a - gain, Oh
C A D7 Am7
Ba-by make me know you love me so an' then, Let's
G Em
Twist a-gain like we did last sum-mer, Yea, Let's
Am7 1 D7 G C D7 Am7/D
Twist a-gain, like we did last year. Come on let's
2 D7 G G7
like we did last year. Come

MOVE IT

Words and Music by
IAN SAMWELL

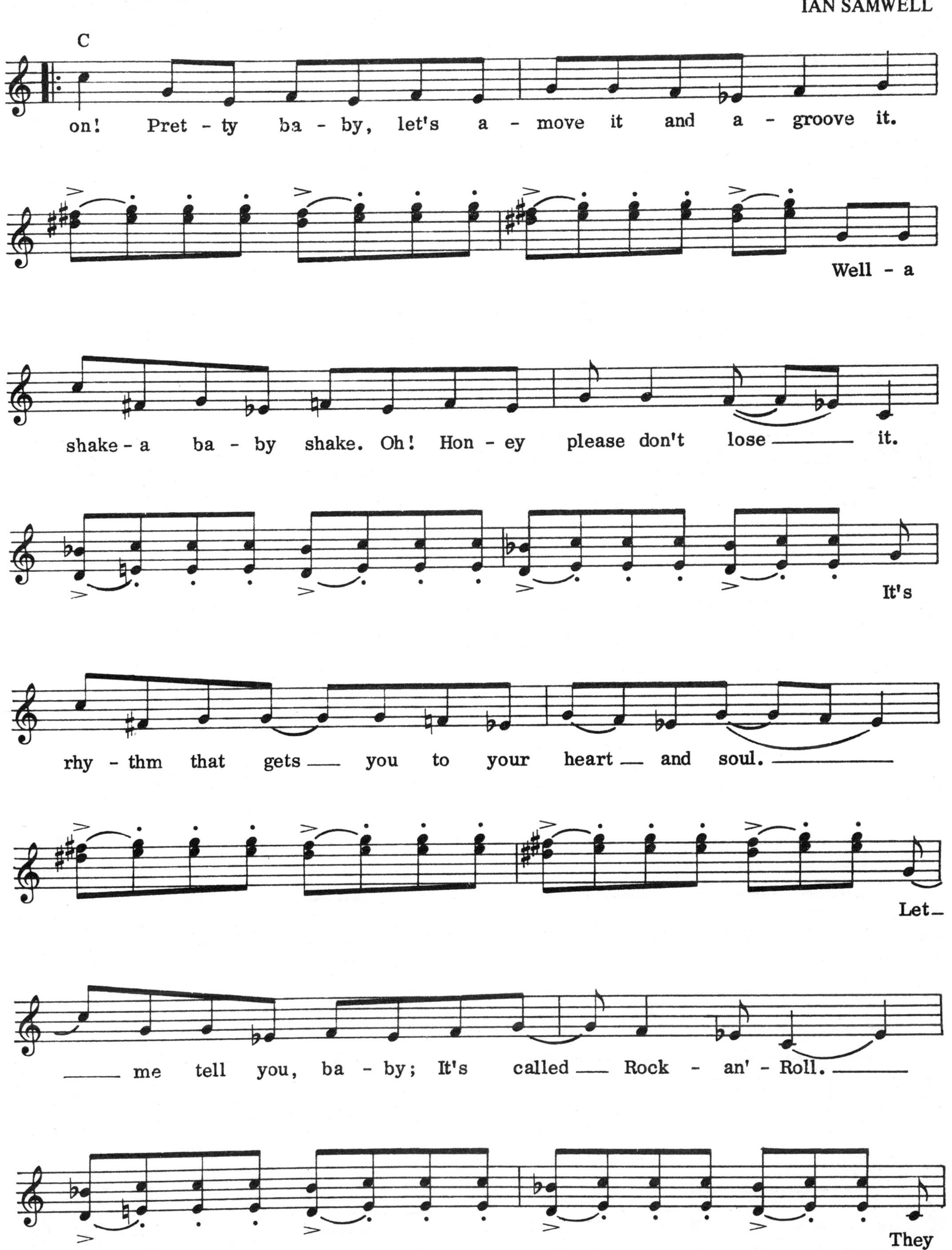
C
on! Pret - ty ba - by, let's a - move it and a - groove it.
Well - a
shake - a ba - by shake. Oh! Hon - ey please don't lose it.
It's
rhy - thm that gets you to your heart and soul.
Let
me tell you, ba - by; It's called Rock - an' - Roll.
They

F7
say it's gon - na die: Oh! Hon - ey - bee, let's face it;
They
C
just don't know what's a - go - in' to re - place it.
Bal - lads and Ca - lyp - sos, they've got no - thing on
F7
real Coun - try mu - sic that just drives a - long.
C
1
Come
2
Oh! Hon - ey move it.

BLUE SUEDE SHOES

Words and Music by
CARL LEE PERKINS

F
Well, it's one for the mon-ey, two for the show, three to get read-y, now

Bb7 F
go, cat, go! But don't you step on my blue suede shoes.

C7 F / Bb7 /
You can do an-y- thing— but lay off of my blue suede shoes. —

F F
Well, you can knock me down, — step in my face, —
Burn my house, steal — my car,

slan-der my name all ov - er the place; —
drink — my li-quor from my old fruit jar; —
Do an - y - thing that you

Bb7
want to do, — but uh - uh, hon-ey lay off of my shoes. — Don't you

F C7
step on my blue suede shoes. You can do an-y - thing — but lay

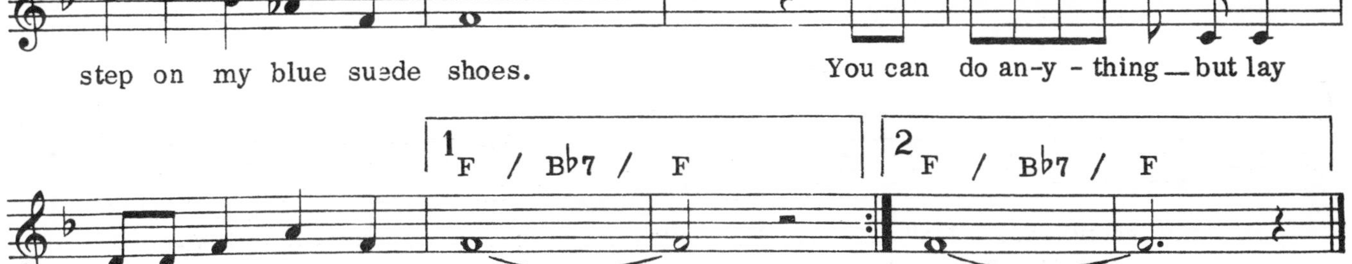
1 F / Bb7 / F
2 F / Bb7 / F
off of my blue suede shoes. —
shoes. —

Medley 10

MA (HE'S MAKING EYES AT ME)

Words by SIDNEY CLARE
Music by CON CONRAD

G7 C
"Ma" he's mak-ing

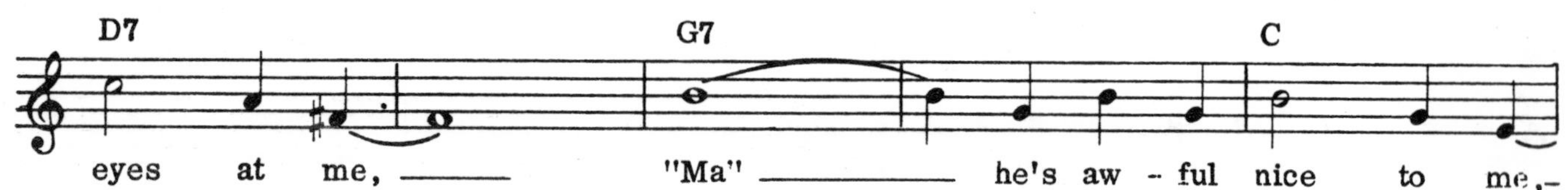
D7 G7 C
eyes at me, "Ma" he's aw - ful nice to me,

C G7
"Ma" he's al - most break-ing my heart,

C G7 C
I'm be - side him, Mer-cy let his con-science guide him, "Ma"

D7 G7
he wants to mar - ry me, Be my hon - ey

C G7 C G7 C
bee, Ev - 'ry min-ute he gets bold - er, Now he's lean-ing

G7 D7 G7 C
3
on my should-er, "Ma" He's kiss-ing me. So what do you

WHAT DO YOU WANT TO MAKE THOSE EYES AT ME FOR?

Words and Music by
JOSEPH McCARTHY, HOWARD JOHNSON
and JIMMY V. MONACO

G7
C
F
want to make those eyes at me for, When they don't mean what they

C
G7
Dm7
G7
say? They make me glad, They make me sad, They

D7
G
3
make me want a lot of things I've nev - er had. So what do you

G7
F
want to fool a - round with me for? You lead me on and then you run a-

E
F
3
F°
F
- way. But nev - er mind, I'll get you a-lone some night and then you'll

G
3
G°
G
3
sure - ly find, you're flirt-ing with dy - na-mite, So what do you want to make those eyes at

Dm7
G7
Dm7
G7
C
C7
me for, When they don't mean what they say?

I REMEMBER YOU

Words by JOHNNY MERCER
Music by VICTOR SCHERTZINGER

I re - mem-ber you, You're the one who made my dreams come
true a few kiss-es a - go.
I re - mem-ber you, You're the one who said "I love you
too," I do, did-n't you know?
I re - mem - ber too, a dis - tant bell, And stars that
fell like rain, out of the blue.
When my life is through, And the an - gels ask me to re-
- call, The thrill of them all, Then I shall
tell them I re - mem - ber you. He's got the

0557

HE'S GOT THE WHOLE WORLD IN HIS HANDS

Arranged by
CECIL BOLTON and CHRIS ELLIS

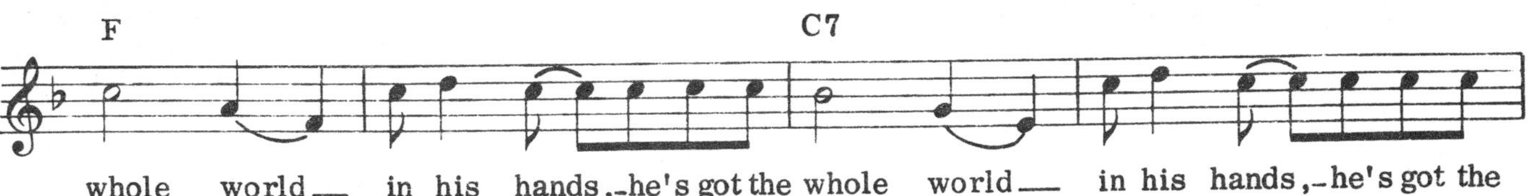
F
C7
whole world — in his hands, – he's got the whole world — in his hands, – he's got the

F
C7
whole world — in his hands, – he's got the whole world in his hands. — He's got the

F
C7
wind and the rain — in his hands, – he's got the wind and the rain — in his hands, – he's got the

F
C7
wind and the rain — in his hands, – he's got the whole world in his hands. — He's got the

F
C7
whole world — in his hands, – he's got the whole world — in his hands, – he's got the

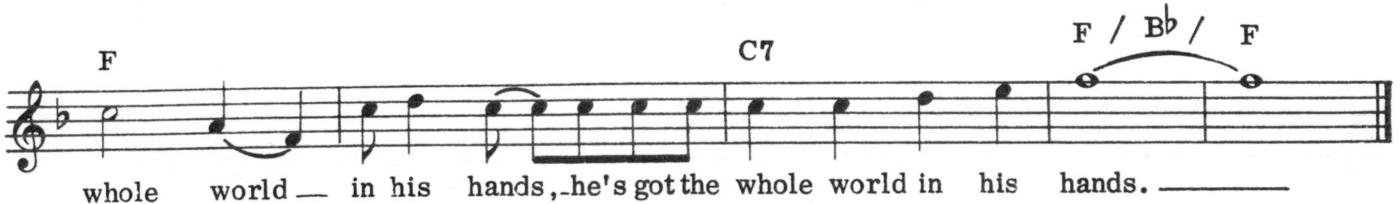
F
C7
F / B♭ / F
whole world — in his hands, – he's got the whole world in his hands. —

Medley 11

BANANA BOAT SONG

Words and Music by
ERIK DARLING, BOB CAREY
and ALAN ARKIN

C
Hill and gul- ly rid - er, Hill and gul-ly, — Hill and gul -ly rid - er,
C
Hill and gul-ly. — Day o, Day o, Day light come and I
G7 C C
wan-na go home. — Day o, Day o, Day light come and I
G7 C C F C
wan - na go home. — Well, I'm load-ing the ba -na-na boats all night long, —
C G C
Day light come and I wan-na go home. — Hey ! All of the work - men
G7 C G7 C
sing this song, — Day light come and I wan-na go home. —
C G7 C
Day o, Day o, Day light come and I wan-na go home. —
C G7 C
Day o, Day o, Day light come and I wan-na go home. — We

SLOOP JOHN B.

Arranged by
CECIL BOLTON and CHRIS ELLIS

F Bb F Bb
sailed on the Sloop, John B., My grand - far - ther and
hoist up the John B sail, See how the — main-s'l's

F C
me, 'Round Nas - sau town we — did roam. —
set, Send for — the cap - tain — a - shore, —

C7 F Bb
— Drink - ing all night, — we got — in a fight, —
— Let — me go home! — Let me — go home. —

Bbm F C7
— I feel so break up, — I want — to go

1 F C7 2 F
home. — So home. — Mi - chael

MICHAEL ROW THE BOAT

Arranged by
CECIL BOLTON and CHRIS ELLIS

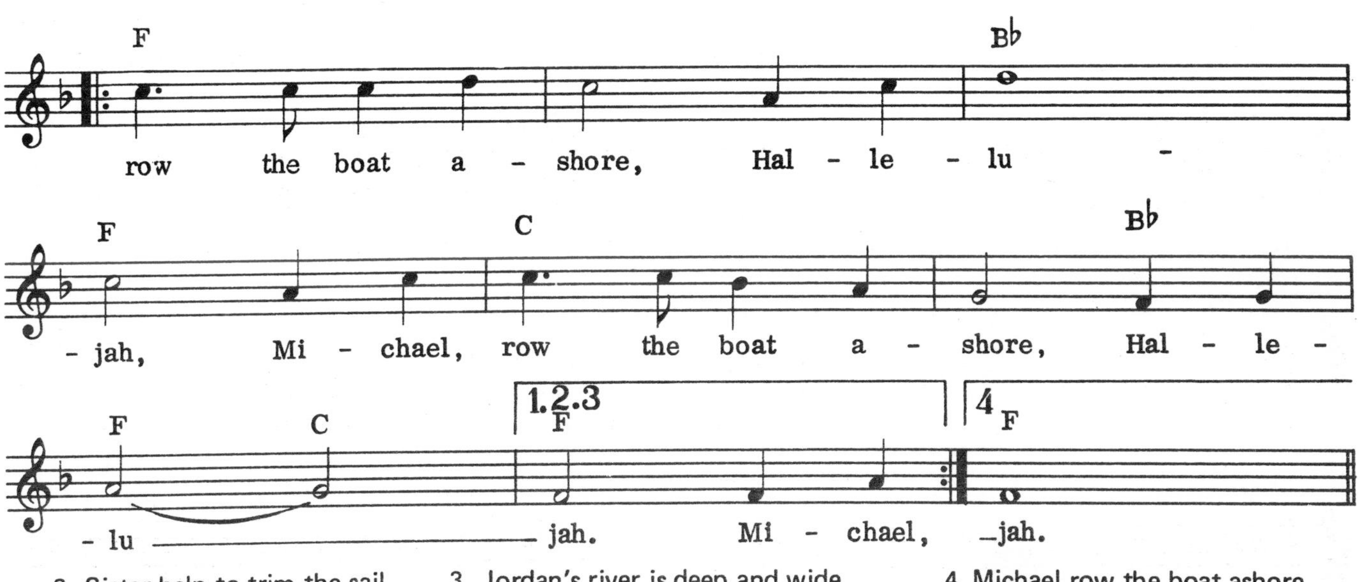
F Bb
row the boat a - shore, Hal - le - lu -
F C Bb
- jah, Mi - chael, row the boat a - shore, Hal - le -
F C 1.2.3 F 4 F
- lu — jah. Mi - chael, — jah.

2. Sister help to trim the sail,
Hallelujah,
Sister help to trim the sail,
Hallelujah.

3. Jordan's river is deep and wide,
Hallelujah,
Meet my mother on the other side,
Hallelujah.

4. Michael row the boat ashore,
Hallelujah,
Michael row the boat ashore,
Hallelujah.

YELLOW BIRD

Words by ALAN BERGMAN and MARILYN KEITH
Music by NORMAN LUBOFF

F E F D7 Gm7 C7 F
Yel - low Bird, up high in ba-na - na tree.
F E F D7 Gm7 C7 F
Yel - low Bird, you sit all a-lone like me.
B♭ F C7
Did your la - dy frien' leave de nest a-gain? Dat is ve - ry sad,
F B♭ F
make me feel so bad. You can fly a-way, in the sky a-way.
C7 F F
You more luck - y than me! I al - so have a
Gm7 C7 F
pret-ty gal, She not with me to - day. Dey all de same, de
Gm7 C7 Gm7 C7 F
pret-ty gal, Make dem de nest, den dey fly a - way.
Dm7 G7 F E F E
Yel - low Bird, Yel - low
F E F E♭7 G7
Bird, Yel - low Bird.

ISLAND IN THE SUN

Words and Music by
HARRY BELAFONTE and LORD BURGESS

C F G7
Oh, Is - land in the sun, Willed to me by my
C F
fath - er's hand, All my days I will sing in praise of your
VERSE
G7 C C
for - est wat - ers, your shin - ing sand. This is my is - land
F G7 C
in the sun, Where my peo-ple have toiled since time be - gan,
C Dm7 C
I may sail on man-y a sea, Her shores will al - ways be
Dm7 C C F G7
home to me. Oh, Is - land in the sun, Willed to me by my
C F
fath-er's hand, All my days I will sing in praise of your
G7 C C
for-est wat - ers, your shin-ing sand.
F Dm7 G7 C

Medley 12

SINGING THE BLUES

Words and Music by
MELVIN ENDSLEY

Well I
nev - er felt more like sing-ing the blues, — 'cause I nev-er thought — that
nev - er felt more like cry -ing all night, — 'cause ev - 'ry-thing's wrong — and
I'd ev-er lose — your love, dear, Why'd you do me this way? —
noth- ing ain't right — with - out you,
Well, I You got me sing-ing the blues. — The
moon and stars no long- er shine, the dream is gone I thought was mine, There's
noth - ing left for me to do but cry —
o - ver you. — Well, I nev - er felt more like run-ning a - way, — but
why should I go — 'cause I could-n't stay — with - out you,
You got me sing - ing the blues.

HAPPY BIRTHDAY SWEET SIXTEEN

Words and Music by
NEIL SEDAKA and HOWARD GREENFIELD

F
Bb
Gm7
C7
Tra la la la la — la — la — la la, Hap-py Birth-day Sweet Six - teen.
F
A7
1. To - night's the night — I've wait - ed for, —
2. What hap - pened to — that fun - ny face? —
Dm
F7
Be - cause you're not a ba - by an - y - more.
My lit - tle tom - boy now wears sat - ins and lace.
Bb
B♮o
F
D7
You've turned in - to the pret - ti - est girl I've ev - er seen. —
I can't be - lieve my eyes; — you're just a teen - age dream. —
G7
1
C7
Hap - py Birth - day Sweet Six - teen. —
Hap - py
2
C7
F
C7
Birth - day Sweet Six - teen. — When you were on - ly six, —
F
C7
I was your big broth - er, Then when you were ten, —
F
D7
We did - n't like each oth - er. When you were

D7 Gm
thir - teen ___ you were my fun - ny val - en - tine. ___ But

C7 Gm7
since you've grown up your fu - ture is sown up, From now on you're

C7 F A7
gon - na be mine; So, If I should smile ___ with sweet sur - prise,

Dm F7
___ It's just that you've grown up be - fore my ve - ry

B♭ B♮° F
eyes. You've turned in - to the pret - ti - est girl I've ev - er

D7 G7 C7 F D7
seen. ___ Hap - py Birth - day Sweet Six - teen. ___

BIMBO

Words and Music by
ROD MORRIS

CHORUS
G D7
Bim - bo, Bim - bo, where ya gon - na go - e - o? Bim - bo, Bim - bo,
D7 G G G7 C
what-cha gon - na do - e - o? Bim - bo, Bim - bo, Does your mom-my know, ___
C D7 D7 G Am7 / / D7
___ That you're go-in' down the road to see a lit-tle girl-e - o? ___

VERSE
G C A7 D7
Bim - bo is a lit - tle boy who's got a mil - lion
G C A7
friends, And ev - 'ry time he pass - es by, they
D7 G D
all in - vite him in. He'll clap his hands and
D
sing and dance, and talk his ba - by talk, With a
D A° A7
hole in his pants and his knees a - stick-in' out, he's just big e - nough to
D7
walk.
CHORUS
G
Bim - bo, Bim - bo, where ya gon-na go - e - o?
D7 D7 G G G7
Bim - bo, Bim - bo, what-cha gon-na do - e - o? Bim - bo, Bim - bo,
C G° D7
Does your mom-my know That you're go - in' down the road to
D7 G 1 Am7 / D7 / 2 G
see a lit - tle girl- e - o?

Medley 13

RED SAILS IN THE SUNSET

Words by JIMMY KENNEDY
Music by WILHELM GROSZ

F 3 Dm7 3 Gm7 3 C7
F 3 F7 B♭ B♭m 3 F
Red sails in the sun - set, 'Way out on the sea,
Gm7 3 C7 Gm7 C7 3 F
Oh, car - ry my lov'd one home safe-ly to me.
F 3 F7 B♭ B♭m 3 F
He sail'd at the dawn - ing, all day I've been blue,
Gm7 3 C7 Gm7 C7 3 F
Red sails in the sun - set, I'm trust-ing in you.
B♭ B♭m 3 F Gm7 C7 3 F
Swift wings you must bor - row, Make straight for the shore.
B♭ B♭m 3 F Dm7 G7 3 C7
We mar-ry to - mor - row, And he goes sail-ing no more.
F 3 F7 B♭ B♭m 3 F
Red sails in the sun - set, 'Way out on the sea,
Gm7 3 C7 Gm7 C7 3 F Dm7 C7
Oh, car-ry my lov'd one home safe-ly to me. I found my

BLUEBERRY HILL

Words and Music by
AL LEWIS, LARRY LAWRENCE STOCK and VINCENT ROSE

thrill on Blue-ber-ry Hill, On Blue-ber-ry
Hill, when I found you. The moon stood
still, on Blue-ber-ry Hill, And lin-gered un-
-til my dreams came true. The wind in the
wil - low played love's sweet mel-o - dy, But all of those
vows we made were nev-er to be. Tho' we're a -
- part, you're part of me still, For you were my
thrill, on Blue-ber - ry Hill.

I'M IN LOVE AGAIN

Words and Music by
ANTOINE DOMINO and DAVE BARTHOLOMEW

G Gm G G Gm G
Yes it means I'm in love a - gain, Had no lov - in' since
C7 C
you know when. You know I love you, yes I do, And I'm
D G Gm G
sav - in' all my lov - in' just for you. Need your lov-in' and I
G Gm G
need it bad, Just like a dog when he's go - in' mad.
C7 G C7 C D
Hoo-ee ba-by hoo - ee. Ba - by won't you give your
G Gm G
love to me. Ee - ny mee-ny mi - ney mo,
G Gm G Gm G C7 G
Told me you did-n't want me 'round no more, Hoo-ee ba-by
C7 C D
hoo - ee, Ba - by don't you let your dog bite me. You

AIN'T THAT A SHAME

Words and Music by
ANTOINE DOMINO and DAVE BARTHOLOMEW

G
made me cry when you said Good -
G C7
- bye, Ain't that a shame! My tears fell like
G C7 C9
rain, Ain't that a shame!
C7 D7
You're the one to blame. Oh
G G
well, good - bye, al - though I'll
G C7
cry, Ain't that a shame, My tears fell like
G C7
rain, Ain't that a shame!
C7 G
You're the one to blame.

Medley 14

SEE YOU LATER ALLIGATOR

Words and Music by
ROBERT GUIDRY

no chord

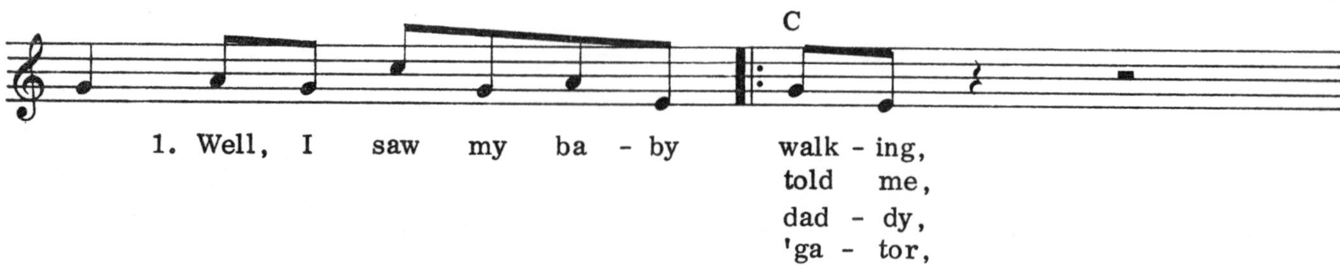
C
1. Well, I saw my ba - by walk - ing,
told me,
dad - dy,
'ga - tor,

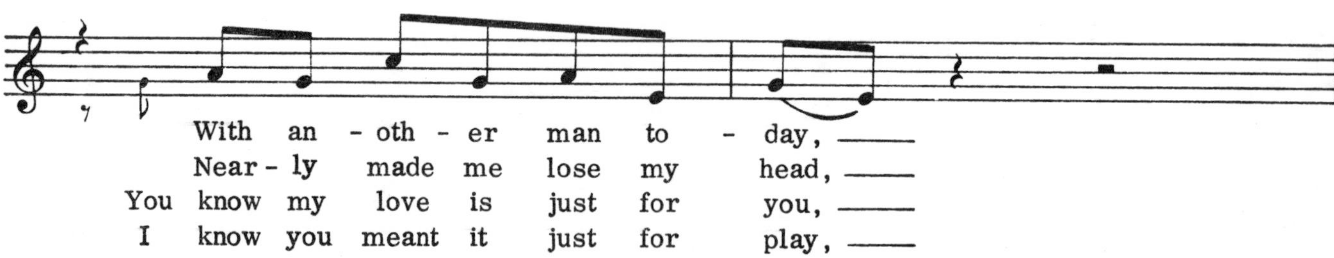
With an - oth - er man to - day, ___
Near - ly made me lose my head, ___
You know my love is just for you, ___
I know you meant it just for play, ___

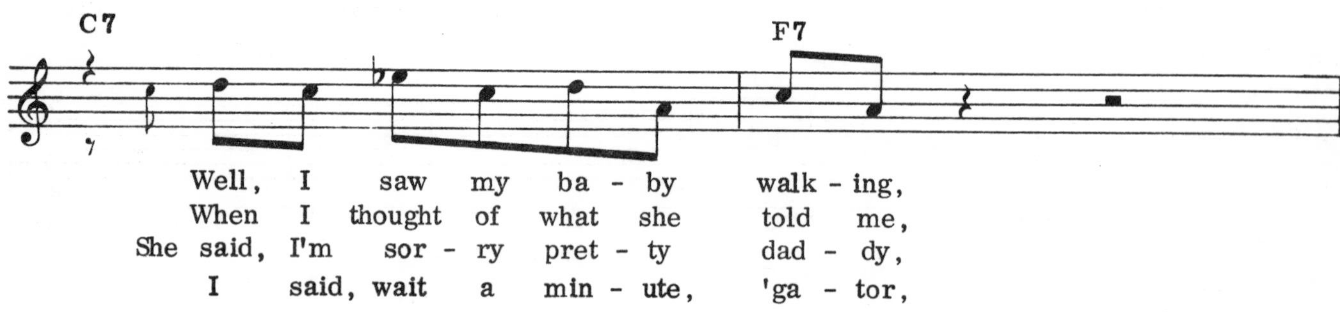
C7
F7
Well, I saw my ba - by walk - ing,
When I thought of what she told me,
She said, I'm sor - ry pret - ty dad - dy,
I said, wait a min - ute, 'ga - tor,

C
With an - oth - er man to - day, ___
Near - ly made me lose my head, ___
You know my love is just for you, ___
I know you meant it just for play, ___

G7
When I asked her what's the mat - ter,
But the next time that I saw her,
Won't you say that you'll for - give me,
Don't you know you real - ly hurt me,
C
This is what I heard her say.
Re - mind - ed her of what she said.
And say your love for me is true.
And this is what I have to say.
no chord
C
See you lat - er, Al - li - ga - tor,
3
Af - ter 'while — croc - o -
dile; —
C7
F7
See you lat - er, Al - li - ga - tor,
3
C
Af - ter 'while — croc - o - dile, —
Can't you see you're in my
G7
1 - 3
C
way, now,
Don't you know you cramp my style?
no chord
4
C
F
2. When I thought of what she
3. She said, I'm sor - ry, pret - ty
4. I said, wait a min - ute,
style? ————

BYE BYE, LOVE

Words and Music by
BOUDLEAUX BRYAND and FELICE BRYANT

C F C F C7 F
1. There goes my ba - by with some - one new,
ro - mance, I'm through with love,
C7 F
She sure looks hap - py, I sure am blue.
I'm through with count - ing the stars a - bove.
F7 B♭ C7
She was my ba - by till he stepped in,
And here's the rea - son that I'm so free,
F F7
Good-bye to ro - mance that might have been.
My lov - in' ba - by is through with me.
B♭ F B♭ F B♭
Bye bye love, Bye bye, hap - pi - ness, Hel - lo,
F C7 F B♭
lone - li - ness, I think I'm gon - na cry. Bye bye
F B♭ F B♭
love, Bye bye, sweet ca - ress, Hel - lo,
F C7 F C7
emp - ti - ness, I feel like I could die. Bye bye, my love, bye
1 F C7 F 2 F
bye. I feel like I could die. 2. I'm free from bye.

ROCK AROUND THE CLOCK

Words and Music by
MAX C. FREEDMAN and JIMMY DAKNIGHT

F
3
One, two, three 'o - clock, four 'o - clock rock, Five, six, sev-en 'o - clock

3
eight 'o - clock rock, Nine, ten, e - lev-en 'o - clock

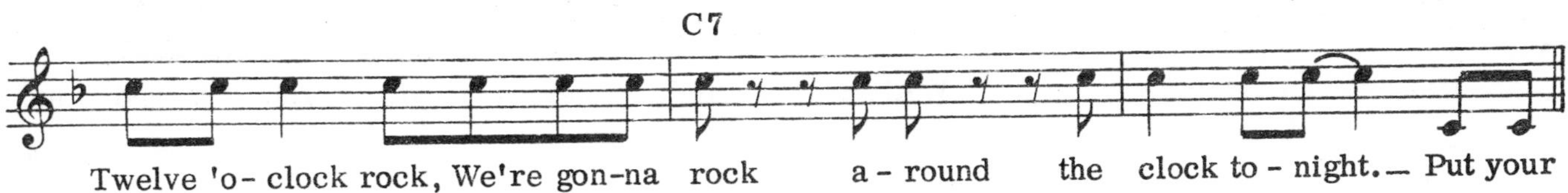
C7
Twelve 'o- clock rock, We're gon-na rock a - round the clock to - night. Put your

F
glad rags on and join me hon, We'll have some fun when the

F7
B♭
clock strikes one, We're gon - na rock a - round the clock to - night, We're gon-na

F B♭ F7
B♭
F
G7
rock, rock, rock, 'til broad day - light, We're gon-na rock, gon-na rock a - round

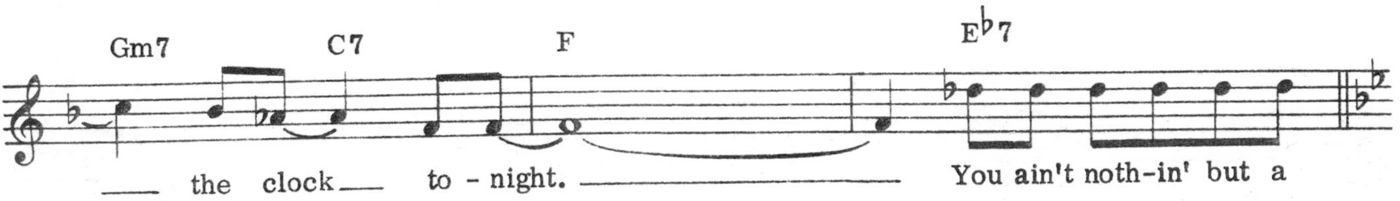
Gm7
C7
F
E♭7
the clock to - night. You ain't noth-in' but a

HOUND DOG

Words and Music by
JERRY LEIBER and MIKE STOLLER

Bb
Hound Dog, cry - in' all the time.
Eb7
You ain't noth - in' but a Hound Dog, cry-in' all the
Bb
F7
time. Well, you ain't nev-er caught a rab - bit and you
Eb7
Bb
ain't no friend of mine. When they said you was
Bb
high - classed, Well, that was just a lie,
Eb7
When they said you was high - classed, Well, that was just a
Bb
F7
lie, Well, you ain't nev-er caught a rab -bit and you
Eb7
Bb / Eb7 / Bb / / C7
ain't no friend of mine. Well, it's

BLUE SUEDE SHOES

Words and Music by
CARL LEE PERKINS

F
one for the mon-ey, two for the show, three to get rea-dy, now
B♭7 3 F
go, cat, go! But don't you step on my blue suede shoes.
C7 B♭ F / B♭7 /
You can do an-y-thing but lay off of my blue suede shoes.
F F
Well, you can knock me down, step in my face,
sland-er my name all ov-er the place, Do an-y-thing that you
want to do, but uh-uh, hon-ey lay off of my shoes.
B♭7 3 F
Don't you step on my blue suede shoes.
C7 B♭
You can do an-y-thing but lay off of my blue suede
F D Am7 D7
shoes. Let's

LET'S TWIST AGAIN

Words and Music by
KAL MANN and DAVE APPELL

G B7 Em
Twist a - gain like we did last sum-mer, Yea, Let's
Am7 D7 Am7/D
Twist a - gain like we did last year. Don't - cha re-
G B7 Em
- mem - ber when things were real - ly hum-min', Yea, Let's
Am7 D7 G C G
Twist a - gain, Twist-in' time is here. Ee - ah
C G
Round 'n - a - round 'n - a up - 'n down we go a - gain, Oh
C A D7 Am7/D
Ba - by make me know you love me so an' then, Let's
G Em
Twist a - gain like we did last sum-mer, Yea, Let's
Am7 D7 G G7/F
Twist a - gain like we did last year.
C/E Cm/E♭ D7 G

Printed by Watkiss Studios Limited, Biggleswade, Beds. 5/9